# Cancer is a C Word

Written by
**Sunita Pal**

Illustrated by
**Cody Andreasen**

Rebel Mountain Press,
Nanoose Bay, B.C.

What is that C word I hear everyone say?
It sounds like a sickness that won't go away.

People seem upset and sad when that word is said.
Is it like a cut or a bruise, or a bump on the head?

I don't understand what the C word could be.
I'll ask my parents, maybe they can tell me.

"What is the word you're hearing?" asked Dad.
"The word's cancer," I said, then Dad became sad.

"We will try to explain, so come sit down here."
We all sat together and they held me near.

Cancer is a sickness that some people get.
Sadly, it's affected some people we've met.

Can't they get medicine to stop being sick?
Let's get them to the doctor—**quick, quick, quick!**

Cancer patients see lots of doctors for their medical care.
Doctors do their best to help sick kids and adults everywhere.

But how do people get this word that starts with a C?
Wait a minute!
Can they spread their cancer to me?

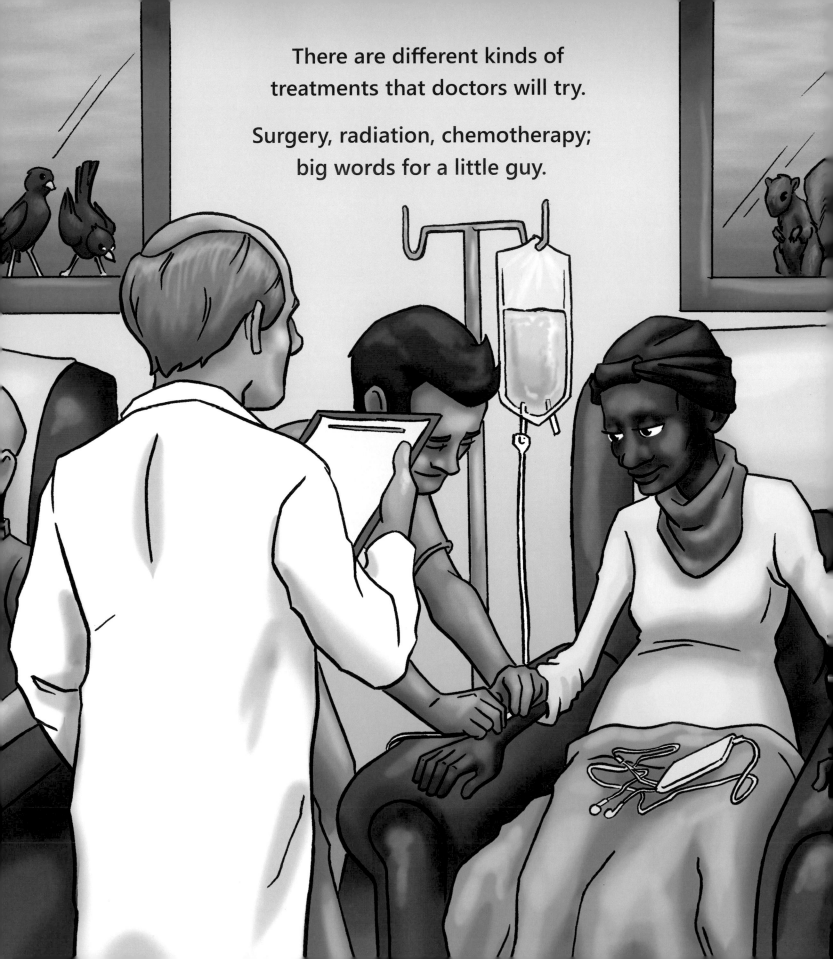

There are different kinds of
treatments that doctors will try.

Surgery, radiation, chemotherapy;
big words for a little guy.

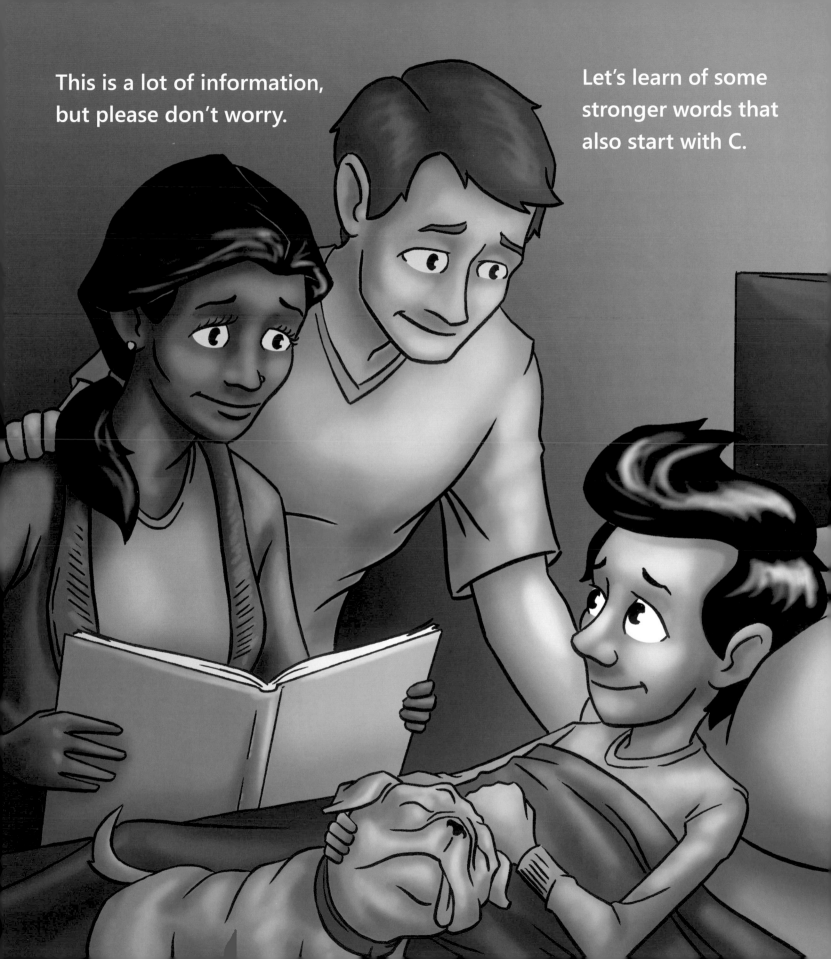

There is a special one called **community.**

A community forms when people come together in times of need.
They are kind to one another, helpful, and do lots of good deeds.

**Cooking** is another C word that will boost someone's mood.

You can help someone who's sick by bringing their family food.

When someone knows
you're there for them,
they see they're not
the only one.

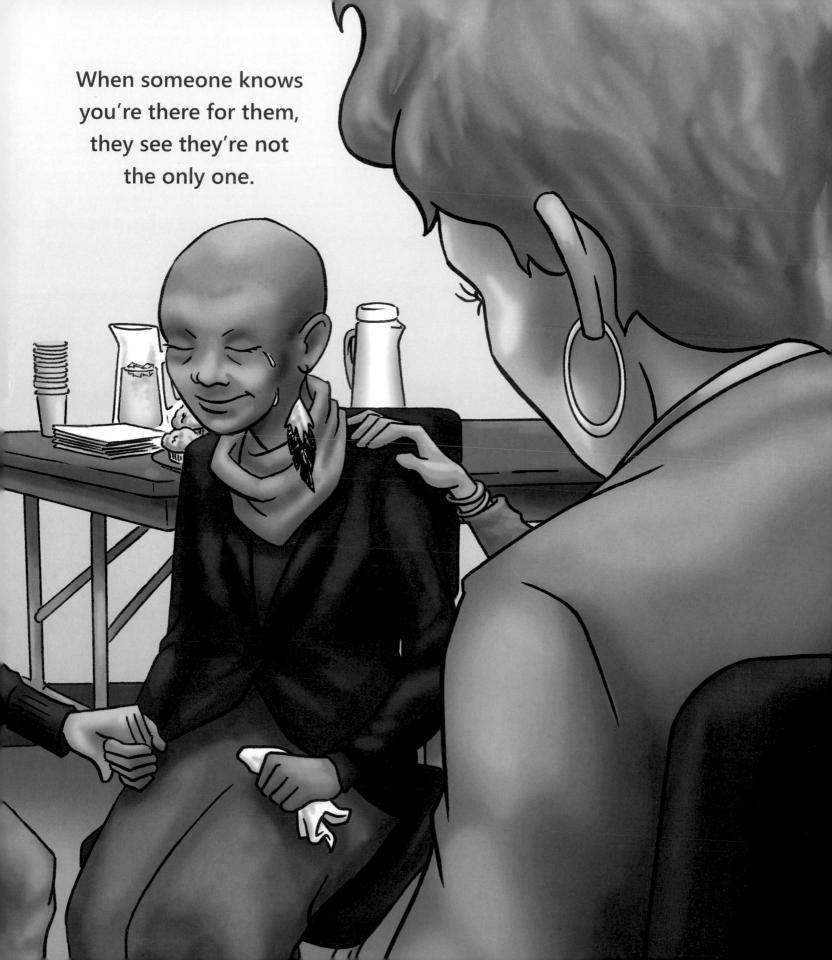

Another C word that means so much to you and me,

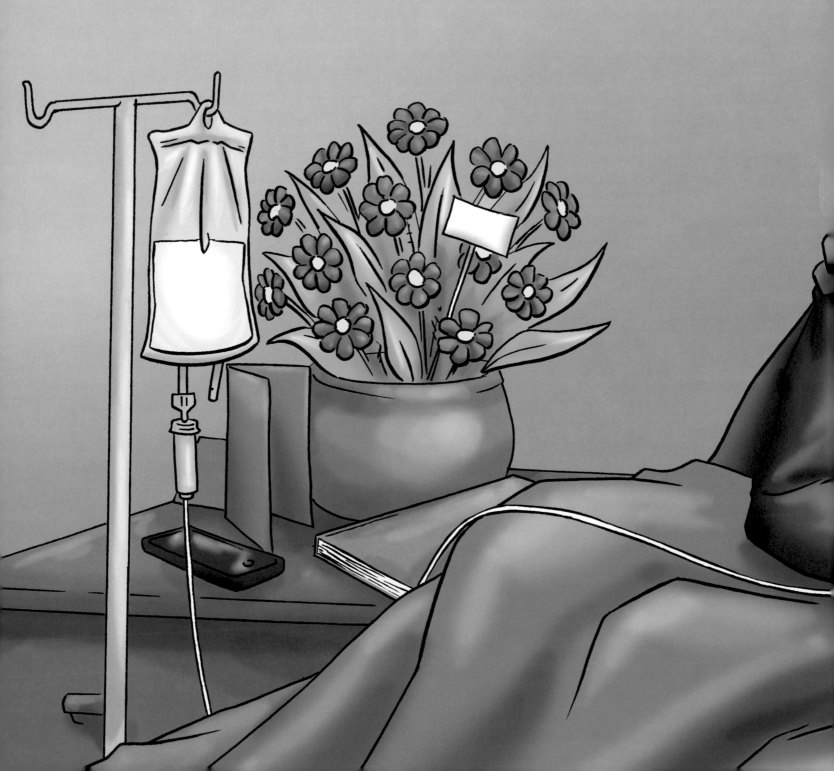

**Cuddling** means to hug your friends and family!

**Caring** is the last C word and one we all need to know.

Helping, friendship, love, and caring is what we all should show!

Cancer is that first C word, the one you did not know.
It means some people are sick and feeling really low.

But remember those new C words that you've just been taught.

They will help lift spirits like you've never thought!

So when we know someone who is sick and sad,
shower them with love and caring—the most they've ever had.

We must stay strong and do our part
to send a warm message
to their heart.

# Glossary of terms

**Affected** – this means someone is feeling a certain way because of something. For example, if someone is affected by cancer that means their body is not acting properly and is sick because of the cancer.

**Cancer** – a disease that is caused when cells are not working the way they should. Cancer can start in one area of the body and spread to other areas.

**Cells** – small parts inside the body that create all living things.

**Chemotherapy** – using chemicals/specially made medicine to try to treat the disease. The medicine is meant to try to destroy the cancer inside the body and stop it from growing. Sometimes it is given through pills, but other times it is given by liquid through a needle. People may feel weak, tired, lose their hair, and have trouble eating when having this treatment.

**Contagious** – when someone has a sickness that can be passed on from one person to another, like a cold or the flu. Cancer is not contagious and you cannot catch cancer from another person.

**Disease** – an illness/sickness that affects a person and causes their body to not work properly.

**Lump** – in this case it means when the cells in your body are not working properly and come together to form a growth inside your body that may feel like a bump under the skin. Some lumps are cancer, but some are not. You do not have cancer just because you have a lump. If someone finds a lump they should have it checked out by a doctor.

**Medical care** – when doctors and other professionals work hard to try and help make people feel better.

**Pass away** – when someone passes away they are not alive anymore.

**Patient** - someone who is receiving medical care.

**Radiation** – the use of x-rays or beams of energy, like a laser, to try and stop the cancer cells from growing. People who have radiation treatment may feel very tired and their skin may get red and itchy.

**Sickness/illness** – when you are not feeling well. It is when your body is not healthy and is not working properly.

**Surgery** – is an operation performed by doctors and other medical professionals.

## Author:
## Sunita Pal

Aside from being a writer, Sunita is also an experienced elementary school teacher. For almost two decades, she has taught from kindergarten to Grade 2 and has even served as school librarian, so she is well versed in what makes for an enjoyable read for the little ones. She also believes in the importance of educating these same little ones on serious subject matters in a meaningful way that is easy for them to understand.

Previous self-publications:

*I Can't Eat That! A story about food allergies and anaphylaxis* (2019),

*My King* (2019),

*My Superhero* (2018),

*My Pets* (2017)

## Illustrator:
## Cody Andreasen

Cody Andreasen is a teacher and artist from Calgary, Alberta. Cody attended the Alberta University of the Arts (formerly ACAD) where he received a BFA in Drawing and the University of Calgary where he received a Bachelor of Education degree. Cody enjoys working in a variety of visual styles including comic books and (recently) puppets. In addition to his art, Cody enjoys making other things, such as his four children whom he created in close collaboration with his wife.

Cancer is a [C] Word
Published by Rebel Mountain Press, 2020

Text copyright © 2020 by Sunita Pal
Illustrations copyright © 2020 by Cody Andreasen

Library and Archives Canada Cataloguing in Publication

Title: Cancer is a C word / by Sunita Pal ; illustrated by Cody Andreasen.
Names: Pal, Sunita, 1978- author. | Andreasen, Cody, 1982- illustrator.
Identifiers: Canadiana 20200217097 | ISBN 9781999241605 (hardcover)
Subjects: LCSH: Cancer—Juvenile literature.
Classification: LCC RC264 .P35 2020 | DDC j616.99/4—dc23

Rebel Mountain Press gratefully acknowledges support for this project by the Province of British Columbia through the BC Arts Council.

BRITISH COLUMBIA ARTS COUNCIL | BRITISH COLUMBIA
Supported by the Province of British Columbia

Printed and bound in Canada by Marquis
Issued in printed format:
ISBN 978-1-9992416-0-5 (hardcover)

ISBN 978-1-9992416-2-9 (EPUB)

Rebel Mountain Press—Nanoose Bay, BC, Canada
We acknowledge that we are located on the traditional territory of the Snaw-Na-Was First Nation

www.rebelmountainpress.com

1  2  3  4  5